REVIVAL FIRES IN CARENAGE

REVIVAL FIRES IN CARENAGE

Chronicles of Spiritual Awakening in the Republic of Trinidad and Tobago

An eyewitness account of the mighty works of God that swept through this quiet community in the 1970s

By

ASHTON DOMINIC MARK

ISBN: Print 978-976-8341-05-1

E-book 978-976-8341-06-8

Bible quotations marked "BSB" are from the Berean Standard Bible, which is in the public domain.

I dedicate this book to the glory of God, the exaltation
of the Name of Jesus Christ—my precious Saviour
and Lord—and to the enduring legacy of those holy
men and women of God whose influence continues to
live on.

With many other words he testified, and he urged them, "Be saved from this corrupt generation." Those who embraced his message were baptized, and about three thousand were added to the believers that day. They devoted themselves to the apostles' teaching and to the fellowship, to the breaking of bread and to prayer. A sense of awe came over everyone, and the apostles performed many wonders and signs. All the believers were together and had everything in common. Selling their possessions and goods, they shared with anyone who was in need. With one accord they continued to meet daily in the temple courts and to break bread from house to house, sharing their meals with gladness and sincerity of heart, praising God and enjoying the favour of all the people. And the Lord added to their number daily those who were being saved. (Acts 2:40–47 BSB)

After they had prayed, their meeting place was shaken, and they were all filled with the Holy Spirit and spoke the word of God boldly. The multitude of believers was one in heart and soul. No one claimed that any of his possessions was his own, but they shared everything they owned. With great power the apostles continued to give their testimony about the resurrection of the Lord Jesus. And abundant grace was upon them all. (Acts 4:31–33 BSB)

TABLE OF CONTENTS

FOREWORD

Revival Fires in Carenage is a heartfelt journey through the history of God's work in Carenage, drawing parallels with the early events in Acts 2:47. Crafted with meticulous care, the book unveils the Pentecostal move of God in the 1970s, portraying the lives and aspirations of those who built and sustained the church. As a witness to the events described here, and being a core part of the chapters within these venerable walls from 1974 to 1978, I am humbled by the author's depth of research and passion.

Starting from its modest beginnings in 1971, each chapter narrates the elevating stories of clergy, congregants, and community efforts in shaping the church into a spiritual cornerstone. The author skilfully weaves anecdotes and historical records, vividly portraying challenges, triumphs, and the enduring spirit propelling the movement. Readers are invited to experience echoes of hymns, prayers, miracles, and profound moments on this historical journey. A bonus section provides a brief history of

Carenage, fostering a sense of belonging and nostalgia.

Revival Fires in Carenage extends an invitation to readers to connect with the past, embrace the shared legacy, and anticipate unwritten chapters in the sacred narrative of the church. With immense gratitude for those who went before us and hopeful anticipation for the future, I invite you to immerse yourself in the sacred narrative of *Revival Fires in Carenage*.

Frankie Mapp

Servant of Jesus Christ

November 2023

ACKNOWLEDGEMENTS

I extend my deepest, esteemed gratitude to the Almighty God for guiding this work and making His presence felt throughout the writing process. His inspiration and divine intervention have been the driving force behind every word penned in these pages.

I am profoundly thankful for the legacy of the co-founders, the late Minister Rudolph Medina, and the late Minister Evelyn Glaude, whose unwavering commitment to Jesus Christ and invaluable contributions to the divine work laid the foundation for the powerful move of God in Carenage during the 1970s. Though they are no longer with us, their spiritual leadership continues to inspire and guide.

Special appreciation goes to all the members and visitors who played pivotal roles in shaping the spiritual landscape of Carenage. Your names are etched in the history of this work, and your devotion to the cause is eternally acknowledged.

I express heartfelt thanks to the Woodbrook Pentecostal Church and its Men's Fellowship Group for their involvement and support during the growth stages of the ministry. The collaboration, commitment, and shared efforts have left an indelible mark on the community.

A sincere thank you to the contributors of the special messages: Minister Rudolph Medina (1933–2005), Minister Evelyn Glaude (1919–2009), Deaconess Martha John (1913–2003), and Minister Veronica Mason. Your insights and spiritual wisdom have enriched the narrative, providing a deeper understanding of the work of God.

I extend my appreciation to all those whose names may not appear on these pages, but whose prayers, support, and encouragement have been instrumental in bringing this account to fruition. Your contributions have not gone unnoticed.

Lastly, I would like to acknowledge the readers—those who will embark on this thrilling journey through the pages of *Revival Fires in Carenage*. May the spirit of revival captured in these words ignite a flame of inspiration and faith in your hearts.

INTRODUCTION

This book emerged out of the deep desire to share some of the wonderful and profound works of God experienced during His mighty move in Carenage in the 1970s. The intention was singular: to glorify God. However, the path to manifesting this divine narrative was fraught with challenges and spiritual opposition. The journey of this writing project commenced in 2001, but was abruptly halted in 2002 as the foremost leaders who tried to document this great work of God faced relentless spiritual attacks. The initial draft of the book vanished for over two decades. During that time, most of the foundation members fell asleep in the Lord.

Miraculously, copies of the draft resurfaced recently, compelling me to resurrect this literary endeavour. Informed by interviews with co-founders and some foundation members, the manuscript required adjustments after more than two decades. These changes, however, did not tamper with the core text approved by the founders in 2002. Instead, the narrative was further enriched with the addition of more instances of God's wonder-working power, recorded as I felt led by the Holy Spirit.

The completion of this book also stands as a miracle. Resuming work on 10 November 2023, after finding the lost draft, a fast and prayer session with the Jesus Expects All Nations Saved (JEANS) Campus house church community on 13 November 2023 marked a turning point. The writing process accelerated dramatically, culminating in the final draft's completion on 22 November 2023.

With the exception of the brethren from Cedros who came with the founder, I stand as the only remaining foundation member from the inaugural meeting in Minister Evelyn Glaude's home in 1971.

I remained in the work until the end, when Minister Medina left Carenage and moved on to his next assignment. As such, I was intimately involved with most of the activities of the movement, as I continued to share a very close relationship with both leaders during the seven-year period of the work.

I feel quite confident that, had they still been alive, they would heartily have approved of my taking on this project to its deserved conclusion.

In honouring their memory and the extraordinary journey we undertook together, I embarked on this unique endeavour with a profound sense of responsibility. It is my sincere hope that this account, which spans the early days of our humble gatherings to the growth, challenges, and miracles we witnessed, will serve as a testament to the enduring spirit of the work we started. May it inspire and enrich the lives of those who read it, capturing the essence of a time when the divine power and presence of God were manifested in the heart of Carenage.

CHAPTER 1

A BRIEF HISTORICAL LOOK AT CARENAGE AND THE NATIONAL CONTEXT

Against the backdrop of Carenage's dynamic history, characterized by its rich maritime heritage, agricultural roots, and the challenges posed by geopolitical shifts in the 1970s, the work of God in Carenage emerged as a transformative force within the community.

With its name of French origin derived from the practice of "careening" or beaching of sailing vessels for maintenance, Carenage boasts a rich and diverse history. The area is renowned for its picturesque bay, a popular spot for sea bathing and liming (hanging out) throughout the years.

In the early 1970s, Carenage was a close-knit community whose inhabitants, predominantly fishermen and farmers, had their roots in Chaguaramas.

However, the dynamics of the Chaguaramas community changed when the Americans took control of the area as a naval base, resulting in the forced relocation of many residents to Carenage. Notable dates include the US Navy's arrival in Trinidad on 10 October 1940, aboard the USS St. Louis, and the commissioning of the US Naval Base in Chaguaramas on 1 June 1941.

Despite the challenges, Carenage has played a crucial role in shaping Trinidad and Tobago's sports landscape, producing notable personalities in football and cricket, such as Ron La Forest and Bernard Julian respectively. Their stories exemplify the talent and dedication that emerged from this vibrant locale.

In the broader national context, the 1970s were marked by political upheavals, with the Black Power movement and the army mutiny being defining moments. With its diverse population, Carenage found itself amidst these sociopolitical changes while continuing to significantly contribute to the nation's achievements.

In 1976, Trinidad and Tobago made a critical political transition by becoming a republic. Sir Ellis Clarke assumed the role of president, succeeding the former governor-general, and Dr. Eric Williams continued as prime minister.

This transition reflected the resilience and adaptability of the nation in the face of both challenges and accomplishments during the tumultuous 1970s. The historical landscape of Carenage, with its roots in agriculture, fishing, and vibrant community life, mirrors the broader narrative of Trinidad and Tobago's socio-economic and political evolution.

Just as Trinidad and Tobago transitioned into being a republic in 1976, symbolizing political change, the spiritual landscape of the Carenage community also underwent profound spiritual change.

The Pentecostal move of God left an indelible mark on the hearts and lives of those who became part of this spiritual journey. This narrative invites readers to explore the interconnectedness of history, faith, and community resilience. The work of God in Carenage during the 1970s serves as a testament to the transformative power of the gospel of Jesus Christ and the enduring strength of hope and spiritual revival in the midst of societal changes and upheavals.

CHAPTER 2

AN OVERVIEW OF THE REVIVAL

The history of the Pentecostal movement in Carenage is filled with the wonders and miracles of the resurrected Christ. During the early 1970s and beyond, revival fires swept throughout this fishing village, a very strong Roman Catholic community, heralding glorious manifestations of the kingdom of God. Filled with divine wonders, these early beginnings beckon for a continuation of such extraordinary visitations even today. Recognizing the importance of preserving these memories, a committee comprised of some original foundation members emerged with a sacred mission—to document the wonderful work of God that began in 1971.

It is crucial to acknowledge the seeds of Pentecost planted earlier by brethren who initiated various works, including the Church of Christ on Lazare Street, St. James, and the endeavours of Pastor Cecil Lowe. Yet, the pivotal moment arrived in late 1971 when Rudolph Medina, affectionately known as Bro. Roy, accompanied by a company of believers—Maurice Phangu, Steve Agard, Boodoo Gopaul, Kenneth Gobin, and Ashton D. Mark—went to the home of the God-fearing woman Evelyn Glaude, at Mt. Pleasant Street, Carenage.

In that humble abode, an agreement was reached between Evelyn Glaude and Rudolph Medina on a Tuesday in November 1971 to commence a divine work—a work that would, unbeknownst to all, blossom into two full gospel Pentecostal churches 31 years later in the heart of the Carenage Community. The first, Shiloh Pentecostal Tabernacle, located in Crown Trace, nestled in the Cocoa area. The second, The West End Pentecostal Christian Fellowship, found its home on Constabulary Street.

The inaugural meetings unfolded on a Wednesday; in attendance were Rudolph Medina, Evelyn Glaude, Maurice Phangu, Steve Agard, Boodoo Gopaul, Kenneth Gobin, Norbert Hepburn, Ashton D. Mark, Theresa Joseph, Martha John, Bertie Craig, Niceta Ballantine, Sis Gulliver, and Beatrice Baker. From the very outset, God graced His people with His mighty presence, ushering in great rejoicing, joy unspeakable, and glory beyond measure. The focus was unequivocally on Jesus Christ and the atonement, with believers wholly given over to prayer and fasting. The Word of God resonated both within and beyond the home, leading to a series of impactful open-air meetings that reverberated throughout Carenage Village.

The first open-air preachers, chosen vessels of God, included Rudolph Medina, Maurice Phangu, Norbert Hepburn, and Martha John. The Lord, in His infinite grace, continually added to the church those who were being saved, while other believers were led to join and strengthen the work. Witnesses to the early beginnings attested to the powerful, intense, and rich presence of God, coupled with an overwhelming love among the believers. Every service was Spirit-led, marked by anointed worship and the preaching of God's Word.

The work flourished for almost three years before being entrusted to the Men's Fellowship Group of the Woodbrook Pentecostal Church, which evolved into an outstation of the Woodbrook Church. By that time, the congregation had grown to over 55 members, prompting a move from the house to the apartment downstairs to accommodate the expanding membership. This transition did not diminish the power and presence of Jesus among the believers; instead, it widened the doors for an even greater, evident outpouring of God's power. Eventually, the work transcended the confines of the apartment, transforming into the church in the Cocoa area.

The ensuing pages seek to delve deeper into the above summary, encapsulating what foundation members believe to be one of the mightiest Pentecostal works of God in Trinidad and Tobago. For simplicity, the time period is divided into three phases.

Phase 1: The Pentecostal move of God during the house meetings held in the living room of Evelyn Glaude's house.

Phase 2: The Pentecostal move of God during the apartment meetings held in Evelyn Glaude's apartment.

Phase 3: The Pentecostal move of God from Evelyn Glaude's property to the Cocoa. This third phase is entrusted to others more intimately acquainted with that period to be documented at the appropriate time, should the Lord permit.

Given the account's purpose—to capture the work
of this great Pentecostal move of God in Carenage at
Minister Glaude's residence—the focus remains solely
on the first and second stages of the work from 1971
to 1978.

CHAPTER 3

PHASE 1 (1971–1974): GOD MOVES IN HOUSE MEETINGS

Beginnings

November 1971 marked the inception of a spiritual journey led by Ministers Medina and Glaude. Their co-founding of this divine work laid the groundwork for a movement that would leave an indelible mark on the Carenage community. While Maurice Phangu and others were briefly present at the outset, the mantle of leadership firmly rested on the shoulders of Ministers Medina and Glaude, ably supported by a core group of devoted believers.

Fellowship, Fasting, and Prayer

A distinctive feature of this movement was the profound devotion to Jesus Christ that characterized its members. The love of Christ permeated the community, fostering an environment of care and mutual support. The believers were not merely individuals attending services; they were a united body readily giving themselves wholeheartedly to prayer, fasting, worship, preaching, teaching, and acts of benevolence.

The weekly rhythm of activities included a dedicated day of fasting and prayer every Wednesday, spanning from 10:00 am to 3:00 pm. Evening services followed at 7:00 pm, with additional days of fasting and prayer observed on public holidays, and Carnival Mondays and Tuesdays. Rudolph Medina took a central role in conducting these sessions, where he not only imparted the teachings of the Bible but also cultivated a deep love for the Word of God among the believers.

There were two nightly services, and they were marked by fervent prayer interspersed with times of intercession. A unique feature was the inclusion of "Unspoken Requests," allowing individuals to present deeply personal prayer needs without mentioning them. In a remarkable incident, a sister's unspoken request was unveiled through the spontaneous prayer of an intercessor, demonstrating a profound connection with the Holy Spirit.

Testimony Time became a platform for believers to share the miraculous works of God.

Testimonies of healings, deliverances, miraculous provisions, salvations, divine directions, and near-death deliverances abounded. Each testimony showcased the evident, extraordinary power of God.

Healing of Cancer

A sister was healed of cancer, leading to the cancellation of a scheduled surgery. Her testimony became a beacon of hope for others facing similar health challenges, highlighting the miraculous touch of God in matters of life and death.

Casting out Demons

A young man attending one of the prayer meetings received deliverance as believers prayed. The manifestation of spiritual warfare was evident as he fell flat on the floor. This event underscored the reality of the spiritual realm and the authority believers wield in Christ.

Miraculous Provisions

Souls rejoiced over God's provision, recounting instances where their needs were met without having to ask anyone for help. This served as a testament to the Lord's faithfulness in supplying not only spiritual but also material needs.

Divine Directions

Believers shared experiences of divine guidance leading to employment opportunities. One testimony highlighted a job secured through explicit directions given in a dream, which emphasized the Lord's involvement in the practical aspects of life.

Near-Death Deliverances

A sister on her deathbed, anointed with oil and prayed for experienced a near-instantaneous recovery. Her testimony spoke of the tangible power of prayer and divine intervention, demonstrating that God held the keys to life and death.

Supernatural Miracle in the Workplace

One testimony stood out—a brother facing dismissal from his job experienced a supernatural intervention.

After he was fired, an earthquake struck, and in the aftermath the General Manager, once resolute in the decision, retracted the dismissal. The workplace became a stage for God's undeniable presence and sovereignty. This supernatural intervention became a testimony to the divine authority that governed both earthly and spiritual realms. The following is a detailed account of that testimony.

In the midst of his dedication to sharing the message of Christ, this brother encountered a unique situation in his workplace. As an active witness for Christ, he distributed gospel tracts until the administrator advised him to cease such activities on the company's premises. Adhering to this directive, the brother continued to share the gospel with his colleagues during lunch breaks.

Unexpectedly, he was summoned by the General Manager and, in a loud voice, was informed that he had been terminated from his position. Accepting the decision, the brother turned to leave the General Manager's office, only to experience a sudden and forceful earthquake. Surprisingly, as he faced the General Manager, the once stern executive was now trembling, exclaiming, "Earthquake! Earthquake!" Unperturbed, the brother calmly affirmed the seismic event, and as suddenly as it had started, the shaking ceased.

While gathering his belongings to exit the company, he inquired about the earthquake from the General Manager's secretary, who claimed to have not felt anything. Perplexed, the brother questioned his co-workers, and none had sensed the earthquake. Strikingly, it appeared that the seismic disturbance was perceived solely by the brother and the General Manager. Unbeknownst to the brother, the General Manager trailed him around the company's premises. Learning of this from a fellow worker, the brother was informed that the "Boss" was closely observing him.

Soon after, the General Manager returned to his office, and the brother received a call from the General Manager's secretary, summoning him back for a conversation. In a notably humbled tone, the General Manager retracted his earlier decision, instructing the brother to disregard the termination—he was no longer fired. This incident stands as a clear-cut testament to divine intervention in the workplace, where a seemingly firm decision was overturned in the wake of a mysterious and exclusive earthquake encounter.

Preaching the Word of God

Every meeting was marked by a rhema word—a timely and relevant message that brought encouragement, strength, correction, and divine direction. Visiting preachers often attested to an increased anointing, sharing how they were compelled to deviate from their already prepared messages to deliver what God intended for that specific moment. The power of God was unmistakable, and the Holy Spirit held sway over every aspect of the meetings.

The Prolonged Presence

Believers faced the challenge of leaving after the services, lingering on to bask in the tangible and enduring presence of God. The fragrance of His richness and glory persisted, prompting believers to extend their fellowship beyond the formal confines of the meeting place. A favourite scripture, "Then they that feared the LORD spoke often with each other, and the LORD hearkened" (Malachi 3:16 King James Version) encapsulated the continued communion among believers.

The Daily Prayers: A Supernatural Deliverance

Within the fabric of the Carenage Pentecostal movement, Evelyn Glaude emerged as head intercessor, leading a profound prayer movement. Her bedroom transformed into an intercessory sanctuary, where believers gathered daily to engage in fervent prayer. Among the earliest participants were Evelyn Glaude, Theresa Joseph, Ruth Tanis, Ashton D. Mark, Niceta Ballantine, and Beatrice Baker.

One remarkable testimony emanating from these sacred prayer gatherings revolves around Ashton D. Mark. On a specific day, Theresa Joseph, prompted by divine insight, interrupted her daily routine to join Evelyn Glaude in prayer for Ashton, sensing he was under spiritual attack. Ashton recounts his deliverance with awe and gratitude.

"While at work, burdened under an unusual weight apparent to all my co-workers, God opened my spiritual eyes. I witnessed everything transpiring over six miles away. In the vision, I saw Theresa Joseph being directed by God to visit Evelyn Glaude, and together they entered the bedroom—the designated prayer room—petitioning for my deliverance.

"As their prayers commenced, the oppressive weight began to lift. Upon the conclusion of their prayers, I was entirely delivered. My co-workers, astounded by the noticeable change in me, openly discussed my transformation, marvelling at the extraordinary events they had witnessed that day.

"After work, I eagerly attended the daily corporate prayer. Approaching Evelyn's house hours later, there they were—Evelyn and Theresa—waiting for me in the gallery. Playing along, I walked up the stairs, appearing downtrodden. As we greeted each other and discussed my day, I suggested we go inside, and I would share my experiences. Without hesitation, I recounted every detail, from the divine prompting for Theresa to visit Evelyn, their joint prayer session, down to the specific time and attire. The presence of God enveloped us as we praised and gave thanks for His marvellous works. What began as a prayer meeting transformed into a joyous praise and thanksgiving gathering. Glory to God!"

This testimony vividly illustrates the divine intervention and deliverance that unfolded through the dedicated prayers of the Carenage believers, thereby deflecting spiritual attacks and ushering in God's transformative power.

Open-Air Meetings: A Supernatural Commencement of Street Evangelism

In the developmental stages of the Pentecostal movement in Carenage, a pivotal moment unfolded after a period of fasting and prayer. Led by the Holy Spirit, the believers ventured into the streets for an impromptu open-air meeting. This marked the commencement of a series of such gatherings throughout the Carenage community. Divinely guided, this spontaneous initiative attracted crowds, leading to profound decisions for Jesus Christ.

The open-air meetings witnessed the emergence of various male and female preachers, amplifying the fervour of the Pentecostal movement. Notable figures in this phase included Rudolph Medina, Norbert Hepburn, Martha John, and Evelyn Glaude. The preached Word was accompanied by tangible signs, and souls were saved, with God confirming His message through miraculous occurrences.

One remarkable testimony stems from an encounter with a notorious drunkard known as

"Bully," renowned for disrupting religious gatherings. During one such meeting at the intersection of Jones and Abbe Poujade Streets, while Rudolph Medina was fervently preaching, Bully approached him, demanding an explanation of who God is. Carrying a flask of rum in his back pocket, Bully provocatively asked, "Who is in charge here?" Interrupting his sermon, Rudolph Medina responded with conviction, "I am." Bully then issued a threat that unless they could demonstrate who this God is, there would be no meeting. In response, Rudolph Medina summoned the believers to encircle this inebriated disruptor. As he led them in prayer, Bully was supernaturally knocked to the ground by the power of God, experiencing instant deliverance and salvation. Subsequently, he willingly underwent baptism and became a welcomed member of the community of believers, a living testament to the transformative power of God.

Dorcas Class Meeting Material Needs: A Ministry of Compassion and Skill

Beyond spiritual activities, the believers in Carenage, under the guidance of Rudolph Medina, established the Dorcas Class to address the community's material needs and nurture various skills. Theresa Joseph assumed leadership of this class where women of all ages gathered to sew, impart skills, and provide for those in need, irrespective of their religious affiliations. Martha John became the inaugural president of the women's group within the Dorcas Class.

The Dorcas Class expanded its capabilities over time, securing its sewing machine through the generosity of saints. This group's annual display showcased the remarkable handiwork of its members, attracting admiration from women's groups in other churches. Their culinary prowess, especially during Christmas festivities, earned the women's group a reputation for savoury cooking.

The Youths for Christ: A Zealous Generation in Service

Under Rudolph Medina's initiative, and spearheaded by Ashton D. Mark, the youth group exemplified fervour and devotion to Jesus Christ. This intergenerational youth group shattered conventional divides, bringing together young people of different religious beliefs in unified worship and service. The group conducted impactful open-air meetings, with

Saturdays being dedicated to fasting and prayer, and stood out for its commitment to sharing the gospel and engagement in intercession.

As the various groups and activities flourished, the movement approached its second growth phase. The Lord's confirmation of His Word remained steadfast, and the believers continued to navigate the unfolding chapters of this remarkable spiritual journey.

CHAPTER 4

PHASE 2 (1974–1978): GOD MOVES IN APARTMENT MEETINGS

Transitions: A Growing Movement

As the work experienced significant growth, Evelyn Glaude's home no longer had enough room to accommodate everyone. People spilled into every available space—kitchen, dining room, living room, bedrooms, gallery, steps, and yard. What began with a modest group of around nine individuals had rapidly grown into a sizable crowd. Phase 2 of the work marked a pivotal moment—a need for a more expansive venue to accommodate the influx of believers. With thrilling testimonies of healings, deliverances, miracles, and the rich presence of God felt at the meetings, people came from nearby areas and afar to experience this mighty work of God.

A Spiritual Struggle for Space: Spiritual Strategy Over Carnal Means

Consideration turned to the apartment, but a troublesome tenant obstructed progress, disturbing meetings with loud, ungodly songs. Attempts to evict him through conventional means failed, prompting a critical spiritual realization. Initially contemplating disconnecting the apartment's electricity, the group was sharply rebuked by God through His intervention. They were reminded of the spiritual nature of their battle and the potency of their spiritual weapons. Fasting and prayer replaced the initial plan. During the dedicated session, tumultuous noises emanated from the apartment. To their amazement, the tenant had vacated during the prayer, paving the way for the church to occupy the space.

Engaging the Community: The Men's Fellowship Group

Another significant change took place during Phase 2. The work was handed over to The Men Fellowship Group from the Woodbrook Pentecostal Church. As such, they played an increasingly vital role during this phase. Figures such as Bro Greir, Wilfred Lewis,

Edward Pierre, and Cecil Thomas became integral to the unfolding narrative. Notable personalities like the 3Ws—Augustus Williams, Michael Williams, and Fred Williams—contributed, along with guest speakers.

Edward Pierre, aptly known as the "man with the message," undertook the needed construction projects, crafting benches and extending the building to accommodate the growing congregation. He was assisted by Ashton D. Mark and Linwall Gomez.

Enriching Encounters: Midweek Meetings and Sunday Mornings

The midweek fasting and prayer meetings underwent a significant transformative evolution with the inclusion of additional speakers, amplifying the spiritual resonance within the community. Augustus Williams, Wilfred Lewis, Michael Williams, Fred Williams, Brother Greir, Pastor Turnel Nelson, and Joycelyn Nelson graced these gatherings, bringing with them an additional wealth of spiritual insights and teachings, thereby further strengthening the saints.

Among the memorable contributors was the renowned speaker, affectionately nicknamed Brother

"Bitter Cup," who left an indelible mark with his powerful sermon on "Christ Drinking the Bitter Cup." This moment became a significant milestone in the collective spiritual journey, offering profound insights into the sacrifice of Christ on the cross, and serving as a wellspring of encouragement for the believers.

As spiritual progress continued to unfold, Sunday morning services were introduced, marking a new chapter in the community's worship. Pastor Nelson played a pivotal role during these services, initiating the practice of Communion on the first Sunday morning of each month. The observance of the Lord's Supper added a further dimension to the Sunday gatherings, fostering a sense of greater unity and reverence among the believers. The introduction of Sunday morning services became a blessing to the growing church, making possible dedicated times for reflection on Jesus Christ's shed blood and His broken body: the price He paid for our redemption!

Milestone of Transformation: Young Pioneers of Change

Another defining moment in the advancement of the work of the kingdom of God in the Carenage community was when a significant number of esteemed Roman Catholics embarked on a miraculous transformation journey by choosing to leave their church and undergo baptism, administered by Pastor Turnel Nelson. At the forefront of this spiritual revolution stood the young people, vessels through whom God worked mightily.

Under the guidance of the Holy Spirit, Michael St. Louis went to the Catholic Church and became the catalyst for a series of events that culminated in numerous baptisms.

The following is his account of what transpired.

"I was praying and fasting one day. While enjoying a time of prayer, a voice distinctly said, 'Go by the Catholic Church.' I knew it was God, but said to the Lord, 'Let me pray a little more, and then I will go.' I then attempted to pray, but the Holy Ghost didn't assist, and the Lord's voice came again, 'Go by the Catholic Church.'

"I obeyed and went. I met five old women moving chairs and the Lord told me to help them. Through this, I was inside when a question was put to me about the Lord. I answered, and then God took over. After this, I was invited to their charismatic meeting held in Sister Arthur's house. I took my brethren Frankie Mapp, Ashton D. Mark, and others. We spoke the Word to them about baptism. They obeyed and asked to be baptized as the Word says. We referred them to Pastor Nelson in Woodbrook, where they were baptized. After that, we continued having meetings with them, teaching them more perfectly in the way of the Lord."

Thereafter, the young people continued to play a pivotal role in the subsequent discipleship and follow-up endeavours.

Another significant event that took place among the young people was networking with their counterparts from other full-gospel churches; namely, the Carenage Gospel Hall and the Church of God on Carlos Street. The present site of Shiloh Pentecostal Tabernacle was once occupied by apartments; Elu Prince Dillon, a member of the youth group, resided on that very property. The young people met there to fast and pray.

Several years later, aligning with God's plan, the Pentecostal Assembly of the West Indies (PAWI) acquired the property. This is yet another testament to how God utilized the zeal and dedication of the young believers to manifest His mighty works in the community.

Impactful Crusades: Spreading the Message

During this period, the Woodbrook Pentecostal Church organized impactful crusades in Carenage. Dynamic preachers such as Jeremiah Prescod and Bro Moore drew crowds, resulting in a number of decisions for Christ and subsequent water baptisms.

Leadership Transition: A New Chapter Unfolds

As this phase drew to a close, Cecil Thomas took over the reins of leadership from Rudolph Medina, who in turn moved on to serve in ministry at the Nazareth United Holy Church in St. James.

By 1978, as the church shifted its location from the apartment to a new venue in Cocoa, the congregation had expanded to over a hundred members.

The L'Anse Mitan Work: A Prelude to Carenage

Before the commencement of the work in Carenage, prayer meetings were initiated in the home of Cecil and Shirley Thomas, involving members of the Woodbrook Pentecostal Men's Fellowship Group. This spiritual gathering later transitioned to the L'Anse Mitan Village Council. Following a series of co-visits and interactions, the endeavours of these two groups seamlessly merged. Cecil Thomas, alongside Rudolph Medina, Bettie Craig, Wilfred Lewis, Norbert Hepburn, and Brother Greir, played a crucial role in laying the foundation for the subsequent work in Carenage.

Ending with Glory: Overcoming Trials

In closing, like all authentic moves of God, this divine work faced trials, divisions, demonic attacks, and false accusations, both individually and collectively. Through unwavering faith, God remained faithful. Despite many afflictions, the congregation entered the kingdom rule of God, growing and multiplying. Indeed, the light afflictions worked for us a far more exceeding weight of glory. Praise the LORD!

CHAPTER 5

SPECIAL MESSAGES

Introduction

Within this remarkable collection of spiritual wisdom, the founders, and some of the earlier members of the church—Minister Rudolph Medina, Minister Evelyn Glaude, Minister Ashton Dominic Mark, Deaconess Martha John, and Minister Veronica Mason—shared the following impactful messages between 2001 and 2002. Each message serves as a beacon of profound personal experiences, offering spiritual insights and invaluable guidance for the church and its members. This compilation unfolds a spiritual legacy, weaving together the collective wisdom and divine revelations imparted by these humble messengers of faith.

Minister Rudolph Medina—A Journey of Redemption

Minister Rudolph Medina shares his transformative journey, emphasizing the power of God's intervention. From the brink of suicide to a life devoted to Christ, he highlights the importance of prayer, fasting, and utilizing the people God sends. His words inspire patience, resilience, and faith in overcoming challenges.

"One can never know what God can do through you at the beginning of your ministry. Sometimes, it is only by looking back that you get to understand the power and wisdom of God's work in your life.

"I was saved in 1958 by the powerful intervention of Almighty God. It was an Old Year's night, and I felt so hopeless about my life that I decided to commit suicide. So, I got a rope and sat alone in my room, preparing to kill myself. I prayed to God and said, 'Lord, if You are really there, then show Yourself to me.' The next thing I knew was that an awesome presence lifted me up bodily and transferred me to the other side of the room. I began to cry and bawl out loudly as I met face to face with a holy God. My wife Doris and the neighbours rushed in, thinking that someone was beating me. I then asked my wife to get me a Bible, which she purchased for one dollar and forty-four cents. This was indeed a new beginning for me.

"I gave my life over to Jesus Christ and immediately began serving Him by preaching His word throughout my community, so that within three weeks I had gotten a gathering of 17 young men following the Lord with me. I eagerly went back to my friends who knew my terrible drunken lifestyle and shared Christ, despite many afflictions, and they said to me, 'If God could save you, then we got to serve Him.'

"I have been serving God faithfully since that time until now and have been used by God in starting and nurturing many missions. I thank Him for allowing me the privilege to be used by Him in this way. God is almighty and full of wisdom; He is holy and full of love toward us. He desires to work in us and to use us to do His will. One principle that has always proven to work for me is that I would never start a work for God without first spending time in fasting and prayer: God answers prayer. It is also so important in God's work to use the people whom God sends to you and not to bypass your present members to look for outside help.

"I am now 68 years old and still strongly desire to see God's work increase and prosper in our land. I admonish you younger ones to be patient and wait through difficult times. Do not faint nor make rash decisions that may be contrary to God, especially in marriage relationships, because a breakthrough is just around the corner for you.

"I also caution you to be careful of ancestral attacks from forefathers who might have been involved in demonic activities. Denounce all ancestral ties and do not keep curious items such as figurines or pictures, which may act as doors for demonic attacks on you. There are powerful demons sent from hell to uproot believers—do not open doors for them by harbouring hatred, envy, or unforgiveness. Do not commit sexual sins that are against your own body and give Satan a better chance at you. Satan loves it when Christians commit sins: every problem that we face on earth can be linked to demonic activity. Therefore, let us rise boldly in the power of God and defeat the kingdom of darkness. IF WE WANT A BREAKTHROUGH, WE'VE GOT TO RUN THROUGH."

Minister Evelyn Glaude—Walking Through Trials

At 83, Minister Evelyn Glaude reflects on her salvation since 1952. She encourages a deepened commitment to prayer, forgiveness, and restoration within the church. Her message warns against treating returning brethren harshly, emphasizing the need for unity and unconditional love.

"I turned 83 years old in July 2002, and have been saved by my Lord and Saviour Jesus Christ since 1952. I used to visit the Lodge across from my home, which accommodated several churches at the time, each church holding its service on a different day. We had Jehovah's Witnesses, Gospel Hall, Anglicans, Pentecostals, and so on, and I loved going to church even though my husband warned me against joining any full-gospel church.

"I kept going to church but was mindful of the warning that I had received from my husband until I visited the Pentecostal church at Lazare Street, St. James, and got saved by the Lord. I went straight home to my husband and declared to him boldly that I had got saved that day. Ever since, I have been walking with the Lord through many trials and obstacles, a lot of which came from my own husband, who was not saved. I have been blessed by God through my children and grandchildren growing up in the Lord. I have also been blessed by my fellowship with good Christian people, some of whom belong to the Gospel Hall church, such as Sister Tommie and Sister Cedeno.

"I am really burdened by the number of Christians nowadays that are so shallow and unmotivated. They don't support meetings at church, and as soon as the slightest thing happens, they are quick to back out. It seems that you always have to crank them up like an old motor car to get them to do things.

"Give great value to prayer: it is the key to everything. Be more forgiving and always seek to be restored to one another, as brethren care for one another. The devil operates like a boxer as he looks for our weak points and keeps hitting us there over and over again so that we will fall. Do not give in to him but rely on God and pray without ceasing for strength to resist him, and, having done all, to stand.

"I point you to the prodigal son's big brother and warn you not to be like him. For we say that we pray for our fallen brethren to return to the fold, but when they return, we treat them so badly. We shun them; we speak evil of them and remind them of their past sins; this is not good. We will all have to stand before the Lord one day, and it is then that our works will be made manifest as to whether they are approved by God or not."

Minister Ashton Dominic Mark—A Call to Holiness and Evangelism

Minister Ashton Dominic Mark fervently prays for revival—a revival of holiness, love for God, and a passion for lost souls. He calls for a return to reverence and genuine worship, stressing the urgency of evangelism. His message challenges believers to abandon man-made ways and follow God's command to seek the lost.

"My prayer unto God, the Father of the Lord Jesus, my Redeemer, is that we as a people of God, by the Holy Spirit, may experience mighty rushing revivals of holiness, love for God, love for one another, and love for lost souls.

"Let the revival of holiness bring again a genuine sense of reverence for who God is: He is holy and a consuming fire. The Scriptures say that we are to be holy as God is holy. Let us have holy fear whereby we may serve God acceptably, with reverence and godly fear. This is a call to order in an age of disorder.

"Let the revival of love for God bring a greater level of passionate and extravagant worship of God. Let us worship God for who He is, and for His great love toward us. It is written that God is Spirit, and those who worship must worship in spirit and truth. God is seeking for true worshippers.

"Let the revival of love for the lost souls create an army of witnesses and evangelists who will take the gospel of Jesus Christ out into the world. For Jesus came into this world to seek and save those who are lost, and He has sent us to do likewise. Oh! For praying saints once again to take hold of heaven until it touches the earth and floods the people with the glory and power of God, yes, until Christ is formed in everyone and the whole earth is full of God's glory in His saints!

"In order to accomplish these things, God must be God, Jesus Christ must be Lord, and the Holy Spirit must be leading us as believers: that means all man-made and self-made ways of doing things must be totally abandoned. For example, Jesus tells us to GO—seek for the lost souls and tell them the good news. Instead, we are saying invite them to our church buildings.

"Whose words are we to follow? The answer is that we must obey God rather than man. Oh, church of the living Christ, let us arise and go forth together with Jesus Christ, who sent us into the highways, alleys, villages, communities, and nations of this world and do the works of Jesus. Let us do ALL that Jesus Christ commanded us to do.

"For those reading these words who have not yet tasted the word of life—Jesus Christ—who have not yet been born again by receiving Jesus Christ into your life. Begin your journey of intimacy with God as your Father, Jesus Christ as Lord, and the Holy Spirit as your guide by saying the following prayer:

"'Dear God, who made the heavens and the earth, please forgive me of my sins through the blood of Jesus Christ. Lord, thank You for dying in my place and rising from the dead so that I might be saved. I open the door of my heart and receive You, Jesus. Come into my heart, Lord Jesus. Thank You, Lord!'"

Deaconess Martha John—Pressing on in Service

Deaconess Martha John, serving since 1963, urges a new generation to replace the departing elders. She emphasizes the need for a deeper spiritual life, decrying the prevailing carnality among today's youth. Her call to prayer, fasting, and readiness for spiritual warfare resonates as she implores the youth to stay dedicated to the Lord.

"I have been serving the Lord since 1963, and at age 70, I am still pressing on. I have served in almost every department of the church, such as head cook, women's group president, Sunday school teacher, and so on, and at present, though a bit down in health, I continue to serve as a deaconess at the Wesleyan Holiness church, which is conveniently located just over the road from my home.

"The old people are going, but where are the youth to replace us? While you are 'partying,' Christ may come, and what will be your answer then? I observe that our young people are not seeking the deeper life. There is too much carnality, so you depend on what daddy or mummy says for your spiritual guidance and do not know the voice of the Good Shepherd for your own selves. Seek to be filled with the Holy Ghost—there are so many depths with God to be experienced still.

"In the old days, there was a greater yearning for God by young people; there was more dedication, more zealousness, and less carnality than today's youth. Older believers need to counsel youths to stay with the Lord and not to give up. The Lord is able to help us no matter how heavy the burden may be, and His Word will strengthen us to deal with problems and challenges: read it daily.

"Let us not treat our service to God lightly or as a mere facade. Instead, let us approach it with sincerity through earnest prayer and fasting in one accord, as God indeed responds to genuine supplication. Prepare yourselves for spiritual warfare! GET READY FOR WAR! (Ephesians 6:10–18)."

Minister Veronica Mason—The Great Race of Life

In this special message, Minister Veronica Mason imparts profound insights into the spiritual race of life, drawing inspiration from the apostle Paul's exhortation in Hebrews 12:1–2. She skilfully intertwines biblical wisdom with practical encouragement, urging believers to cast aside hindrances, face challenges with courage, and keep their focus on Jesus—the ultimate author and finisher of their faith. As one of the earlier voices among the foundation members, Minister Mason shares timeless truths to guide the reader on their spiritual journey.

"Brothers and Sisters, we are indeed engaged in a race. Paul's exhortation to us as believers is clear: 'Wherefore seeing we also are compassed about with so great a cloud of witnesses, let us lay aside every weight, and the sin that doth so easily beset us, and let us run with patience the race that is set before us; looking unto Jesus the author and finisher of our faith; who for the joy that was set before Him endured the cross, despising the shame, and is set down at the right hand of the throne of God' (Hebrews 12:1–2 King James Version).

"Having just surveyed the achievements of past heroes of faith in chapter 11, Paul inspires and challenges us to let them be our example, and to face the contest we are in with the same concentration and endurance.

"We ought to throw off despondency and discouragement and, in spite of persecution, face life with courage and confidence. To fall out or to do otherwise is to encounter the divine displeasure of Almighty God.

"Beloved brothers and sisters, there are moments in this race of life when we may be tempted to consider giving up. However, in verse 2, Paul provides encouragement. As we navigate this journey, let us intentionally fill our minds with thoughts of Jesus and reflect on all that He endured for us. He remains, and will forever be, our perfect example—the author and finisher of our faith.

"We have to know and come to accept that God uses earthly trials and experiences for our spiritual discipline and education. The very fact that these things are happening to us proves that God is dealing with us as His sons and daughters.

"Since we have such a huge crowd of men of faith watching us from the grandstands, let us strip ourselves of everything that slows us down or holds us back, especially those sins that wrap themselves so tightly around our feet and trip us up. So let us run with patience this particular race that God has set before us, keeping our eyes on Jesus, our leader and instructor."

CHAPTER 6

KEY LESSONS AND BEST PRACTICES

Introduction

In this section, I distil crucial lessons and best practices from the transformative experiences documented in this book. These insights—which are adaptable and can be implemented based on each community and church's unique characteristics and needs—offer guidance for contemporary communities and churches striving to achieve similar results, reflecting the wisdom gained from the dynamic Pentecostal movement in Carenage during the 1970s.

Total trust, devotion, and reliance on God: A foundational aspect of the Carenage revival was unwavering trust in God, devotion to Jesus Christ, and reliance upon the leading and guidance of the Holy Spirit.

Best practice: Cultivate a culture of complete trust, deep devotion, and reliance on God in every aspect of the church's life and mission.

Prayer and fasting: Spiritual practices such as prayer and fasting will have a transformative impact.

Best practice: Encourage and organize regular prayer and fasting sessions to strengthen the spiritual foundation of the community.

Proclamation of the gospel: Regular and effective proclamation of the gospel of Jesus Christ is fundamental.

Best practice: Continuously explore and employ effective ways to share the message in the twenty-first century.

Regular Spirit-filled worship services: Engaging and dynamic worship services can strengthen the believers and lead to church growth.

Best practice: Encourage regular fellowship times and overall worship experiences that create glorious and joyful celebrations for God to manifest in glory and power.

Personal testimonies: Supernatural experiences and testimonies create a powerful atmosphere for faith and hope to thrive.

Best practice: Encourage individuals to share their stories and experiences of spiritual encounters, creating a transformative and authentic environment.

Adaptability: Being adaptable to changing circumstances and needs is crucial for growth.

Best practice: Regularly assess, adjust, and implement the necessary changes to meet the evolving needs of the community and the church.

Collaboration and networking: Collaborating with other churches and groups can enhance the reach and impact of the church's ministry.

Best practice: Establish partnerships and networks within the broader community to share resources and support each other.

Youth empowerment: Involving and empowering young people can bring vitality to the church.

Best practice: Allow and encourage youth to take initiatives that cater to the advancement of the kingdom of God and involve them in leadership roles.

Legacy building: Documenting and preserving the church's history contributes to a lasting legacy.

Best practice: Maintain records, publish materials, and celebrate milestones to build a sense of identity and continuity.

Leadership transition planning: Planning for leadership transitions allows for the continuity of the church's mission.

Best practice: Seek out from within the congregation potential leadership succession and mentorship to prepare the next generation of leaders.

CONCLUSION

Contemplating the collective impact of the Pentecostal movement and enduring legacy, one cannot help but marvel at the profound transformative journey experienced by the community of Carenage. The lessons learned, the spiritual practices embraced, and the devotion to God have left an indelible mark on the hearts and lives of those who were part of this extraordinary movement.

As we conclude this chronicle of revival fires in Carenage, it is not truly an ending, but a continuation of the spiritual legacy that has been built. The seeds sown during those fervent days of revival continue to bear fruit, and the echoes of worship and prayer still resonate in the hearts of those touched by the move of God.

May this account serve as both a historical record and an inspiration for future generations, encouraging them to seek God's divine presence with the same fervour and passion. The story of Carenage is a testament to the enduring power of faith, prayer, and community, and it beckons us to embark on our own journeys of spiritual awakening.

As we turn the pages of history, let us not only remember but also carry forward the flame ignited in Carenage—a flame that reminds us of the boundless possibilities when a community is united in faith and seeks the face of God.

EPILOGUE

As we reflect on the journey chronicled in these pages, we are reminded of the transformative power of faith and the enduring legacy of a community touched by the hand of God. The revival fires that swept through Carenage in the 1970s were not merely historical events but a testament to the resilience of individuals, the unity of believers, and the unwavering faith that overcame trials.

The work, born in a small room, expanded beyond walls and became a beacon of light for those seeking solace and salvation. The testimonies of healing, deliverance, and spiritual growth are etched into the collective memory of a community that stood witness to the mighty works of God.

The leadership changes, the challenges faced, and the growth experienced all contributed to a narrative of divine intervention and human dedication. The echoes of crusades, special messages, and the voices of the founding members resonate throughout the years.

This book is not just a historical account: it is an invitation to relive the moments when heaven touched earth and lives were forever changed. The epilogue serves as a closing chapter, but the impact of God's work in Carenage reverberates throughout time, leaving an indelible mark on the hearts of those who walked this sacred journey.

May the lessons learned, the miracles witnessed, and the messages shared continue to inspire future generations. The flame that was kindled in Carenage in the 1970s might have taken different forms, but its essence lives on in the hearts of those who carry the torch of faith into the future.

In conclusion, let us rejoice in the faithfulness of God, celebrate the victories, and remember that the work of God is an ongoing, ever-unfolding story. The revival fires might have dimmed in certain chapters, but the embers of faith continue to glow, ready to be fanned into flames once again. Glory to God!

NAMES OF SOME MEMBERS/VISITORS

During the vibrant period of 1971–1978, the Carenage community experienced a profound spiritual awakening. The following individuals played pivotal roles, either as core members or valued visitors, contributing to the remarkable tapestry of the time:

Rudolph Medina, aka Bro Roy (Co-Founder)

Evelyn Glaude, aka Sis Glaude (Co-Founder)

Andrea Lucille Mark

Ann Gomez

Ann Marcelle

Ashton Dominic Mark

Augustus Williams

Brother Barnett

Beatrice Baker

Beatrice Thomas, aka Sis B

Bella Nelson

Benjamin Agard

Bernadette Keels

Boodoo Gopaul

Boysie Wade

John Gour

Carol Mapp

Cecil Thomas

Celena Thomas

Cheryl Isaac

Claudette Scott

Cyril Mc Kie

Daniel Baptiste, aka Louie

Derrick Medina

Dora Wade

Doris Medina

Earl Phillip

Edris Felix

Edward Pierre, aka Man with the Message

Eliza Mc Kie

Elu Prince Dillion

Eric Mason

Eugene John

Eugenia Thomas

Frankie Mapp

Fred Williams

Gemma Abdullah

Gloria Romain, aka Sis Babe

Harold Baker

J.B. Farrell

Jacqueline Henry, aka Jackie

Jane Phillip

Joann Saddoo

Kenneth Gobin

Lennore James

Linwall Gomez, aka Bro B

Marsha Munro

Martha John

Martin Philip, aka Buttie

Marva Munro

Mary Wade

Matthew Mason

Maurice Phangu

Michael St. Louis

Michael Thomas

Michael Williams

Michelle Thomas

Minnie Zamore

Myrtle Felix

Natalie Mark

Nelson James

Niceta Ballantine

Nora Noel

Norbert Hepburn

Norbert Niles

O'Brien Glaude, aka Pape

Olive Charles

Pamela Charles

Peter Felix

Phill Thomas

Phyllis Williams, aka Sis Popolyn

Raymond Saddoo

Rennard Philip, aka Pape

Richard Yearwood

Rita Philip, aka Sis Arthur

Romania Peltier

Rookmin Boodoo

Russell Sutton (the guitar man)

Ruth Tanis

Samuel Phillip

Sandra Baptiste

Selwyn Phillip

Sherma St. Louis

Shirley Thomas

Shirlyn Berkeley

Steve Agard

Steve Charles

Steve Munro

Steve Thomas

Terrance Charles

Thelma Forde

Thelma Kirby

Theophil Joseph, aka Bro Theo

Theresa Joseph, aka Sis T

Uline Peltier

Vashti Kerr-Barnett-Niles

Veronica Mason, aka Sis Vero

Wayne Glaude

Wayne Joseph

Wilfred Lewis

Yvonne Thomas

This list reflects the diverse and dedicated individuals who contributed to the flourishing spiritual community during that significant era. But note: this list may not be exhaustive and may be missing some names.

A CLOSING REFLECTION ON REPENTANCE AND REBIRTH

I now send you, to open their eyes . . . that they may receive forgiveness of sins and an inheritance among those who are sanctified by faith in Me. (Acts 26:17–20)

Therefore produce fruit that proves your repentance. (Matthew 3:8)

Though you do not see Him now, you trust Him; and you rejoice with a glorious, inexpressible joy. (1 Peter 1:8)

Embarking on the path of repentance is a profound journey, marked by transformative signs, emotions, and actions. The Scriptures guide us through this spiritual metamorphosis, emphasizing the tangible manifestations of a heart turned toward God.

At the very moment of repentance, you may or may not experience any feelings or emotions. But sometime afterward, you will experience the signs of being born again: becoming a new person with a new heart, a new joy, a new peace, and a new spirit. You will be like a newborn baby with longings to feed on the milk of God's words.

These are some of the results of true repentance:

- Praying (talking and listening) to God
- Reading, listening to, and meditating upon God's Word—the Bible
- Confessing and forsaking sins
- Making restitution and amends for past sins against others
- Hating the sins you once loved
- Baptism in water
- Baptism in the Holy Spirit
- Being in fellowship with other believers
- Attending fellowship meetings
- Hunger and thirst after righteousness
- Giving charity (alms)
- Fasting
- Loving and serving others as Christ loved you
- Witnessing and testifying of Jesus Christ to others

A word of caution on emotions: while feelings and emotions may come and go in your life, your walk with God is not hinged upon nor dependent on how you feel. Rather, it is based upon loving and trusting in God. The main "sign" of repentance is a changed heart.

The journey of repentance is an ongoing transformation, guided by faith, love, and the indwelling Holy Spirit, leading us to a life of holiness and righteousness.

ABOUT THE AUTHOR

Ashton Dominic Mark, a Minister in the Jesus Expects All Nations Saved (JEANS) House Church Movement, hails from Jones Street in Carenage. Alongside his wife, Dr. Paula Thomas-Mark, and their children—Dr. Atia Mark, Julian Brathwaithe, Asha Mark, Maria Brathwaite, Arnelia Mark, and Janelle Mark—he weaves the tapestry of his life's journey.

Having devoted his professional career to the United Nations Development Programme (UNDP) from 1979 to 2005, where he worked at the Port of Spain office in Trinidad and Tobago, Minister Mark transitioned to ministry in the JEANS House Church Movement in 2009. His spiritual journey began in 1969, making him the first in his family to embrace salvation and undergo a transformative experience with Jesus Christ. With over 50 years of devotion to Christ and ministry, including a missionary venture in Kitale, Kenya, during the early 2000s, Minister

Mark has served the kingdom of God in various capacities.

Acknowledging God's saving grace in his life, Minister Mark recognizes the profound impact on him of generations within his family, including his mother, Andrea Lucille Mark.

Following his dedicated service at the UNDP office, Minister Mark assumed the role of office administrator at Ephraim Medical Enterprises Limited (EMEL), his wife's medical practice, where he continues to serve faithfully.